Sumer
Is Icumen In
OUR EVER-CHANGING LANGUAGE

HOWARD GREENFELD
Sumer
Is Icumen In
OUR EVER-CHANGING LANGUAGE

CROWN PUBLISHERS, INC.
New York

Also by Howard Greenfeld

GYPSIES

BOOKS: FROM WRITER TO READER

THEY CAME TO PARIS

10 9 8 7 6 5 4 3 2 1

The text of this book is set in 12 point Electra.

Library of Congress Cataloging in Publication Data
Greenfeld, Howard.   Sumer is icumen in.
Bibliography: p. 66   Summary: Traces the evolution of the English language over
the centuries, discussing the influence of other languages upon it, euphemisms, and
slang. 1. English language—History—Juvenile literature. [1. English
language—History] I. Title.   PE1075.G67   420'.9   78-15166
ISBN 0-517-53225-5

To Barbara A. Bannon

Contents

Sumer
Is Icumen In
OUR EVER-CHANGING LANGUAGE

Introduction: Man's Most Astonishing Creation

Washington Irving's Rip Van Winkle, hero of one of the most popular stories in American literature, slept for twenty years during the eighteenth century. When he awoke, he found that many alarming changes had taken place, some of which undoubtedly concerned changes in the language spoken by his friends and neighbors.

To show simply what could happen to our contemporary language over a similar, relatively short period of time, let's pretend that a modern Rip Van Winkle goes to sleep in 1931.

1

Forty-six years later, he awakens. A great deal has changed, but before he leaves his room to discover these changes, he picks up a magazine which he finds by his bed. It is dated November 1977. He turns the pages and comes to a section headed RECORDINGS. He begins to read. At the very beginning of the article, he comes to a number of words that are totally unfamiliar to him: *stereo, solid state, reel-to-reel tape, LP.* . . . Still groggy, he reaches for his dictionary, *Practical Standard Dictionary of the English Language,* Funk and Wagnalls, 1931. It is just where he left it forty-six years before. He leafs through the dictionary eagerly, but can find no definitions for any of the words he has just read.

Back to the article. . . . The writer mentions identifying every tune and "lick." A *lick,* he remembers, and finds confirmation of in his dictionary, is a "stroke of the tongue . . . as much as can be taken up by the tongue at one stroke . . . a stroke, blow, or a whack." What has this to do with music?

More puzzled than ever, this contemporary Rip reads of a songwriter's personal "hang-up." The dictionary says that *hang-up* is a verb meaning, in some cases, to "postpone or delay."

Things just get worse as he reads on. Something is labeled a "schlock" anthem. No such word in the dictionary. "Women's-lib material" is referred to. It's impossible for him to figure that out. There is mention of a "soul" album; he knows perfectly well what *soul*

2

means, but in that context? Then, "teenybopper." *Teeny* means very small or tiny, he knows, but what could a "bopper" be?

When he comes to a sentence saying that a "song doesn't poop out," and learns from his dictionary that to *poop* means "to strike a vessel on the poop or stern," he is tempted to go back to sleep.

This story serves only to illustrate that our vocabulary changes drastically—often, and over a very short period of time. Many of the words that our Rip didn't understand, such as *stereo, solid state, reel-to-reel tape,* and *LP,* are words that have come into the English language through need: technical advances in the field of recorded music have been such that new words were essential to identify them. After all, even the machine on which the recordings have been played has been, within this century, known as the *talking machine,* the *Victrola,* the *gramophone,* the *record-player,* and the *phonograph—* before the word *stereo* came into use.

Other words that puzzled Rip came into our language in other ways. Some, such as *lick* and *soul* and *hang-up* and *teenybopper,* are examples of modern slang. *Schlock* is a Yiddish word that worked its way into the English language after Rip went to sleep, just as many other foreign words did. *Women's lib,* even if he had guessed that *lib* was an abbreviation for *liberation* and not for *library* or *librarian,* as his dictionary stated, would have meant nothing to him. The idea was certainly around in his time, but the term itself came into our language later, because of newly recognized social and psychological needs.

This contemporary Rip Van Winkle would certainly give a great deal of thought to the changing language in the weeks following his awakening. For most of us, however, language is so much a part of our daily lives that we tend to take it for granted. But to have an idea of its importance we need only imagine our lives without it. How would we express our thoughts, our wishes, and our feelings to one another? In prehistoric times, man used pictures—called hieroglyphics—for this purpose. Ancient Egyptians made drawings of objects—a sun, a moon, a snake, or a bird—on the walls of caves. Later on, idea pictures, or ideograms, were used. For example, a picture of an owl might represent wisdom, or a drawing of a house could mean security or comfort. But these means would be inadequate for us in communicating more complicated or abstract thoughts. We could cry or whimper or scream or grunt; we could point to objects, shake our heads, twist our faces into grimaces, or pull our lips into smiles . . . but we couldn't clearly and accurately say what we thought or felt or wanted.

There would be no conversation or exchange of ideas. Without language, there could be no literature—no poetry, no novels, no philosophy. We would be unable to study history or science or communicate any kind of knowledge to one another. There would be no government, and modern business could certainly not be conducted without words. As Lytton Strachey has written, "Perhaps of all the creations of man language is the most astonishing." For that reason, it is of great interest to know how our language has developed over the centuries.

In any study of the history of a language, it is important to remember that language is very much the creation of human beings, an essential tool fashioned by people to serve their purposes and meet their needs when they occur and as they change.

Some languages, such as Sanskrit and Gothic, are known as dead languages today because they are no longer used—we know of them only through written records—and are therefore incapable of growth. Living languages, on the other hand, are those which continue to grow, which flourish through use, and are gradually modified by changing circumstances. They reflect life and society, and the development of a language is most often the result of political, social, and cultural changes in any given society.

Such is the case with English, our language, which was first brought to the island of Britain from the continent of Europe about fifteen hundred years ago by bands of Teutonic invaders. The changes brought about since that time—proof of the language's vitality—have been so great that eighth-century English is totally incomprehensible to us today.

There have been changes of all kinds—in spelling, pronunciation, and vocabulary, as well as in grammar and syntax—but the language of our ancestors has gradually become more understandable to us. We cannot today read the eighth-century epic poem *Beowulf* without special study, but we know the meaning of "Sumer is icumen in," from a thirteenth-century song, and by the time we come to Chaucer, who wrote in the fourteenth century, we can understand what he meant when he wrote: "And smale foweles maken melodye,/That slepen al the night with open yë"—though his spelling and pronunciation are far different from ours.

In Shakespeare's time, a few centuries later, the language came still closer to ours, though many words still had different meanings, and Shakespeare's contemporaries pronounced his verses quite differently than does a twentieth-century Shakespearean actor. Even the eighteenth-century poet Alexander Pope spoke what sounds now like a comic Irish dialect. In his famous "Good nature and good sense must ever join;/To err is human, to forgive divine," the word *join* is meant to rhyme with *divine*, making it sound like "jine."

From *Beowulf* to Chaucer to Shakespeare to Pope, the English language has proved to be highly adaptable and durable. The British colonization of America added further to its riches, and today it is a uniquely powerful means of communication throughout much of the world.

Of the three billion people in the world today (speaking about three thousand different tongues), an estimated three hundred and fifty million use English as their first language. Another estimated four hundred million know it as a second language, one that they are able to use when their own doesn't serve them.

Even those figures don't give a full idea of the importance of English today. Approximately three-quarters of the world's mail is written in English, half of the world's newspapers are printed in English, three-fifths of all radio stations transmit their programs in English, and over half of all technical and scientific publications are written in English. English is the mandatory second language of airlines all over the world and is rapidly replacing French—which itself replaced Latin in the seventeenth century—as the language of international diplomacy and conferences. The influence of English is even considered dangerous in some places; in France, for example, the government is doing its best to see that its people replace with French equivalents the many English words—such as *snack*, *weekend*, and *self-service*—that are becoming part of every Frenchman's vocabulary.

The reason for the astounding influence of English throughout the world is clear. The importance of a language is, above all, dependent on the cultural and economic power of the people who speak it, and for a few hundred years first British and then American economic, military, and cultural strength has dominated many areas of the world. The British have for centuries been adventurous explorers and traders; they have established colonies on many continents, colonies which are now part of the British Commonwealth. Americans, through two world wars in this century, have been sent all over the world, and since the end of the Second World War American businesses and businessmen have been a powerful force in many countries. They have, naturally, brought their language with them wherever they have gone. American science and technology, too, have in large measure dominated during the twentieth century, so that the English language has provided new words, widely used throughout the world, for new products, concepts, and methods.

The purpose of this book is to make us think about our language: how it grew, just what it is today, and some of the ways in which we use it. It is divided into two parts. The first part consists of a brief history of English—tracing its development from its birth until the time we can begin to call it Modern English, the time when the language was, for the most part, fixed and stabilized.

The second part is a miscellany of the ways in which the language has been enriched since its basic rules and vocabulary were established—through adoption of words from other languages, through creation of words, through euphemisms, and through slang. It also touches on the often surprising changes in the meanings of individual words throughout their history, and the changes in the English language when it was imported into America.

The whole is meant to be no more than an introduction, leading to an awareness of the joys of our language. It is hoped that it will serve as a stimulant to further study in an area of learning which is of fundamental importance to our lives.

Our Linguistic Ancestors

Each of the world's languages belongs to a family of languages. There is a Semitic family, which includes Hebrew and Arabic; a Ural-Altaic family, which includes Finnish, Hungarian, Turkish, and Mongolian; a Sino-Tibetan, which includes Chinese, Thai, Burmese, and Tibetan. Our language, English, belongs to the Indo-European family, which is called that to give an idea of the geographical span of this widespread family, whose members include languages spoken throughout most of Europe and in some parts of Asia.

10

Languages which could be considered cousins of English—some more distant than others—include not only living languages such as French, German, Spanish, Italian, Dutch, and Persian, but also dead languages, which are no longer spoken, such as Sanskrit, Ancient Greek, and Latin. These are all identified as related languages because of the similarities of many of their basic words. The English *father*, for example, is *pitr* in Sanskrit, *pater* in Latin and in Greek, *pidar* in Persian, *vader* in Dutch, V*ater* in German, *padre* in Italian and in Spanish, and *père* in French. So, too, our English *three* is *tri* in Sanskrit, *tres* in Latin and in Spanish, *treis* in Greek, *thri* in Persian, *drie* in Dutch, *drei* in German, *tre* in Italian, and *trois* in French. These aren't exactly the same, but they are close enough to show us that all of these tongues were descended from a single source, a prehistoric parent language, no longer spoken, which is called Indo-European.

There are no written records of this forgotten language; all we know about it and about the people who spoke it has been learned through scholarly studies of the offspring languages. These studies have revealed that our linguistic ancestors lived as a single group in the late Stone Age—until between 3000 and 2000 B.C. But where? In searching for their geographical roots, scholars first agreed that they must have lived in an area that still speaks an Indo-European tongue. This area was narrowed down by a careful study of those words that we

11

know these languages have in common. Indo-European tongues have common words for snow and winter and for the beaver, the wolf, and the bear, animals which flourish in cold climates. There are no common Indo-European words for palm trees or for any tropical plants, nor are there common words for lion, tiger, or camel, animals found in warmer climates. Because of this, it was deduced that our distant ancestors lived in a cold climate. There are no common words for sea or ocean or surf, so these people lived away from the coast. There is a common word for honey; since that isn't found in Asia, Asia was eliminated as the homeland of our ancestors. A word for beech exists in Indo-European languages, and that tree is found only in central Europe—so the area in Europe was narrowed down. On the basis of this linguistic evidence, it seems likely that the original speakers of Indo-European made their home in the plains of what we now call southern Russia.

Studies of their common vocabulary have taught us much about how these people probably lived. The family was important to them, and they spent a great deal of time out-of-doors. It seems they lived largely in wooden huts, but they had no windows—there are no common words for window. They had a form of government, and they had some idea of religion. They knew how to spin and weave, so we can guess how they clothed themselves. We know they ate a kind of bread, since there were words for plow, wheat, yeast, mill, and dough.

At one point, they left their native land in central Europe and dispersed throughout Europe and parts of Asia. Perhaps they had to leave in search of food, or maybe they were merely adventurous or curious. They must have been strong since they imposed their language wherever they went.

This language, however, changed considerably in the course of their travels and settlements. Leaving their land in separate waves at different times and in groups of varying size, they were influenced in varying degrees by the people among whom they traveled or settled. From one parent tongue, many tongues developed. In time, members of the same family could not understand one another.

The Early Years
of Englisc

If a man stopped you in the street and breathlessly an-
nounced, "Se cyning friỗ nam," you would certainly
think he was using a foreign language to say, "The king
made peace." But he wouldn't have been; he would have
been speaking English—Old English, a tongue spoken
many centuries ago, but English nonetheless.

Old English does indeed sound foreign to our ears
today, yet it was the first stage in the development of
our language. That language developed and flourished
on the island of Britain, but it wasn't born there. Before

14

English was brought to the island, the language of Britain was Celtic and the people were known as Celts. These Celts were happy speaking their own tongue; even a long occupation by the powerful Romans did little to change their linguistic ways. But in the fifth century Britain was invaded by tough and determined tribes from northern Europe who not only overwhelmed them physically but also imposed a new language upon them. These tribes were the Angles and Saxons and Jutes. They all spoke a kind of German, known as West Teutonic, and by the seventh century so did the Celts of Britain. The emerging English language—then known as Englisc, taking its name from the Angles—was a typically Germanic tongue, more similar to today's German than to the English spoken today. But this Germanic language was only the basis for the new language; soon other tongues made their influence felt. First there was Latin, when missionaries from Rome came to the island to convert the inhabitants to Christianity. As they succeeded in this task, they also added many of their own words to the Germanic vocabulary of the English, words dealing with education and literature and, above all, religion. The English language was beginning to borrow words from other tongues when necessary; it has never stopped doing this.

Then came the Vikings, courageous but merciless tribes, also from northern Europe, who began to invade the island by the middle of the ninth century. At first, they merely robbed homes and plundered churches and monasteries and then went home; but later many liked what they saw, and large numbers of them settled on the island of Britain. By the eleventh century, they were amalgamated with England; subdued and absorbed by their new land, they were one with the Anglo-Saxons. They were great sailors and they had an intricate system of law, so very many sailing and legal terms, Viking in origin, came to enrich the English language. When there were conflicts between the two tongues, they were resolved. For example, *skirt* in Scandinavian and *shirt* in English originally meant the same thing—a long, smock-like garment. So a compromise was worked out: the Scandinavian form came to mean the lower part, and the English the upper.

The two languages blended together and a simplification and clarification of English resulted. In order to facilitate understanding between the two coexisting peoples on the island the complications and ambiguities in the English language had to be, and were, eliminated. The result was an increasingly concise language.

By the middle of the eleventh century, Old English was still largely Teutonic, but with powerful Latin and Scandinavian elements. It is a language that only specialized scholars can understand today, and only about 15 percent of all Old English words have found their way into Modern English. Nonetheless, among those words that have survived are many that make up the backbone

16

of our language: *man*, then *mann*; *child*, then *cild*; *house (hus)*; *strong (strang)*; *eat (etan)*; *good (god)*; *drink (drincan)*; and *live (libban)*.

Because it was already a rich and useful tool to serve man in his need to communicate with his fellow man, the English language was off to a powerful start.

Middle English

By the middle of the eleventh century the Scandinavians and the Anglo-Saxons were one, and their languages had been successfully blended together. But in the year 1066 this newly developing language was threatened by an invading and conquering force that spoke a foreign tongue. That English not only survived but profited from this challenge is a proof of its strength and vitality.

These powerful invaders were the Normans, who lived across the English Channel in northwest France. Under their leader, William the Conqueror, they not only de-

18

feated the English, they overwhelmed them. For many generations after the Norman Conquest the language which dominated the island was that of these invaders—Norman French. Yet English never disappeared. It remained the language of the peasants and of the working classes, so that, though it lost its importance as a social and cultural instrument (Norman French was used by the government and by the schools), it continued to be the most widely used means of communication by the majority of the people. In time, too, political and social conditions in their home country forced the Normans to reconsider their role in Britain. Gradually, they came to think of themselves as British rather than French, and by the late fourteenth century, English was again the official language of the island.

But this language, now known as Middle English—to distinguish it from Old English, which preceded it, and from Modern English, which followed it—was in many ways a new language. Its close contact with Norman French added more than ten thousand words to the English vocabulary—English borrowing either the exact French word or slightly changing its spelling. More than 75 percent of these words are still in use today.

These words entered the English language very slowly at first, and then more rapidly after the Normans began to abandon French and use English as their first tongue. The basic everyday words remained English; it was, after all, the Normans who adopted the English language and not the reverse. There was no need for new words for *head, arm, leg, foot, hand, eye, ear, nose,* and *mouth.* By the same token, English had satisfactory words to represent the basic elements of everyday life, such as *eat, drink, sleep, work, play, speak, sing, walk,* and *run*— there was no reason to change these. When the Normans came home at night, they found their houses consisted of everyday terms contributed by the English, such as *room, window, door, floor, step*—and the word *house* itself.

However, the language of the Norman French provided words that the Normans had used for which there were no precise, or satisfactory, equivalents in their newly adopted tongue. These words, so many of them now a part of the English language, reflect the Norman way of life, and those activities in which they excelled.

First of all, since French was for so long the language of the clergy, many religious terms were taken into English. Among these are *religion, angel, prayer, saint, miracle,* and *divine.* Norman supremacy in the areas of government account for the adoption into English of another large group of French words, among them *government, state, nation, people,* and *treaty.* French was spoken in the courts of law, so many English legal terms are derived from that language—*judge, jury, justice, verdict,* and *crime,* to mention only a few. The Normans had controlled the army and navy, so many military terms from French found their place in the English vocabulary.

20

Among these were *army, navy, war, peace, battle, victory,* and *defeat.*

In the years following the Conquest, it was the French-speaking upper class which enjoyed the finer things of life, including high fashion and jewels; therefore, French supplied such words as *fashion, dress, robe, gown, satin, fur, diamond, pearl, ruby,* and *sapphire.* These upper-class Normans had time for recreation, so their words *leisure, dance, melody, music, chess,* and *checkers* were borrowed by the English language. The same was true for many words used in the world of art, such as *painting, sculpture, art,* and *color,* all of which were adopted from the French.

French cooking, then as now, was considered supreme, and many French cooking terms were incorporated into English: *sauce, boil, fry,* and *roast,* for example. Many foods, too, are of French origin, such as *salmon, sardine, sugar, salad, grape,* and *olive.*

If any generalization can be made concerning the overall contribution of the French vocabulary to the English language, it might be said that French provided the refinements while English provided the basic elements of life. English contributed *ox, swine, calf, deer,* and *sheep;* the French cooked them and brought them to the table as *beef, pork, veal, venison,* and *mutton.* The relatively simple breakfast was English; the more elaborate *dinner* and *supper* were French. The common *baker, miller, brewer,* and *smith* are English, while *tailor* and *barber* (whom we use only on special days) are French.

In this period of linguistic development—never before or since in its history did the English language change so radically—that followed the Norman Conquest, words came into our language from many languages in addition to French. Many of these came from the Latin—more technical terms such as *genius, polite, rational,* and *index.* Other words were borrowed from Dutch, Flemish, and German—*deck, lighter, easel, landscape, freight,* and *etching,* to give a very few examples. English was continuing to exhibit that extraordinary ability to borrow and make use of words from other tongues that has made it such a rich and vital means of communication.

There is no better proof of the richness and power of expression of Middle English than the writings of Geoffrey Chaucer, a short example of which shows how that language—used six hundred years ago—already closely approached the English we use today.

> A Knight ther was, and that a worthy man,
> That fro the tyme that he first bigan
> To ryden out, he loved chivalrye,
> Trouthe and honour, fredom and curteisye.
> Ful worthy was he in his lordes werre,
> And therto hadde he riden (no man ferre)
> As wel in Cristendom as hethenesse,
> And ever honoured for his worthinesse.

This excerpt from *The Canterbury Tales* is comprehensible to any reader of Modern English—only a slight additional effort is necessary to understand it all. The spelling is often different, but as the words are pronounced their meaning is clear. Chaucer also wrote *koude, condiciun, seyd, contree,* and *armee,* spellings no less logical than our own. Some words need explanation—*werre* is war, *ferre* is further, *hethenesse* is heathen parts. But the English language, enriched by its contact with other tongues and again simplified by the necessity of two foreign peoples communicating with one another, was fast approaching maturity.

Toward Maturity

Think of the English language as a growing child. By the end of the Middle English period, in the late fifteenth century, it was several centuries old, but it was still changing and developing. Born of a linguistically mixed family, it had come into contact with other tongues, had been influenced by them, and had borrowed from them. It was already a beautifully expressive tongue, but it was in some ways unformed and in some ways still inadequate.

It was still unformed largely because this one language

24

consisted of four principal, distinct dialects, each spoken in a different region of the country. The variations in these dialects were many—in spelling, in grammar, and in usage. For example, the word *loves* was used in the north, *loven* was used in the two dialects spoken in the center of the country, and *loveth* was the term common in the southern dialect. There was no authority to say which was the correct, the standard English, and even if there had been, there would have been no way to spread this English throughout the island of Britain, for literature—which would have been that authority—was passed on only by means of costly handwritten manuscript books, a luxury available to none but the privileged few.

This confusion, which threatened to delay the orderly development of the language, came to an end with the invention of printing from movable type, which enabled many copies of any one book to be printed at a relatively low cost. This revolutionary process was invented in Germany by Johann Gutenberg in the middle of the fifteenth century and introduced into England by William Caxton, England's first printer, publisher, and retailer of books.

Caxton's publication, in 1477, of the first book printed on English soil was a major event in the history of the English language. From then on, an unlimited number of copies of any book—identical in content—could be produced and made available to all English-speaking people. In the early years, this was still a small number, for literacy was not widespread, but the number of readers increased when tradesmen, prosperous though not members of the upper classes, were able to give an education to their children.

Caxton's books—about seventy-five of them were published by the end of the fifteenth century—were important because they made one single dialect known throughout the country. The dialect was that of London—because of its location in the center of the country, because of its proximity to the two great universities of Cambridge and Oxford, and because of the city's importance as England's commercial and governmental center. As this London dialect became universally known by means of the printed page, it gradually became the authority for rules of grammar, and through the printed page new words could be disseminated and their use accepted in a relatively short period of time. Books, by establishing tradition and rules, fixed the language in matters of grammar and syntax. Through them local differences were ironed out, and the linguistic chaos caused by local dialects was ended.

Another problem that became apparent was that the English language was still somewhat inadequate as a vehicle for expression of complex, abstract ideas—those found in the Latin and Greek classics which were enjoying great popularity among scholars in Europe during the so-called Revival of Learning in the sixteenth century. These works were available only in their original languages and were therefore the exclusive property of Latin- and Greek-speaking scholars, who felt they could never be properly translated into modern languages. However, many Englishmen who knew no Latin or Greek also wanted to read these great books, and they believed that their own language was potentially rich enough to express any idea, no matter how complex. Their insistence and desire to learn were such that soon translations of these masterpieces of classical literature began to be published in English.

These translations not only opened up new worlds of thought and knowledge to those unable to read Latin or Greek; they also, not surprisingly, helped to expand the English vocabulary.

The scholars had been right. Many of the phrases and concepts written by the classical writers were impossible to translate into English. But instead of dismissing them as impossible to put into English, the translators borrowed words from Latin and Greek to fill in the gaps in the English language. These new words greatly enriched the vocabulary of the latter, to an extent unknown since the time of the Norman Conquest. In fact, it is estimated that as many as ten thousand new words entered our language from the Greek and Latin during the late sixteenth and early seventeenth centuries. Many of these were tried and then discarded, but a very large number survive and are commonly used today.

During this last period of rapid growth and expansion of vocabulary, other words came into English from many other tongues, too—French, Spanish, Italian, and Portuguese among them, so much so that some critics felt this virtual flood of new words was threatening to overwhelm and destroy the English language. These people believed that a large number of these words were unnecessarily obscure—used only to show off the intellectual superiority of those who used them. In many cases this was probably true, but many of these new words were rapidly accepted because there was a need for them. With continued use, they became less exotic and more common. It is hard for us today to think of words like *capacity, fertile, native,* and *relinquish* as being used only to show off someone's intellectual superiority, yet people who used these words were once considered pedantic.

No matter what the critics said about its faults, it is reasonable to state that by the end of the seventeenth century the English language had reached its maturity. If anyone doubts the great power and beauty of this language and its ability to express the full gamut of human emotions, he or she need only read the works of William Shakespeare, who wrote in the late sixteenth and early seventeenth centuries. His vocabulary was relatively small—consisting of approximately twenty thousand words—but by using the basic words of the English language he was able to convey simply and beautifully the most profound thoughts and feelings of mankind. It was Shakespeare who wrote, "How much better is it to weep at joy than to joy at weeping," in *Much Ado About Nothing*, and "All the world's a stage,/And all the men and women merely players," in *As You Like It*. "Love all, trust a few, do wrong to none," is from that great writer's play *All's Well That Ends Well*, and "What's in a name? That which we call a rose/By any other name would smell as sweet" will always be remembered as a part of *Romeo and Juliet*. In these quotations Shakespeare used common everyday words to express thoughts of universal significance. But he also used in his plays and in his poetry many new words, among them *accommodation*, *reliance*, *obscene*, *modest*, *vast*, and *critical*, and he was the first to use colorful, descriptive compounds such as *heartsick*, *long-haired*, and *hot-blooded*. Shakespeare's works remain almost miraculously contemporary today, attesting not only to his genius, but to the remarkable strength of the English language as it attained its maturity.

Taming the Language

Shakespeare's language—as well as his use of it—was glorious. It was also wild and unruly. The great poet and his contemporaries paid little attention to rules regarding grammar or word usage. Conventional grammar, as we think of it today, was disregarded, and words were coined seemingly at random. For the English language, testing its strength not only in England but also in America, where it had been transplanted and altered, it was necessary that this disorganized development be halted—or at least tamed.

One method of accomplishing this was by the creation of grammars, books that establish rules of correct usage that are both logical and reasonable. In these early grammars, common errors were pointed out and disputed points were settled. These latter included the distinctions between *shall* and *will, lie* and *lay, towards* and *toward,* etc.

An even more powerful element in this taming of the language was to be the dictionary. We take dictionaries for granted today; there are so many of them and they are—or should be—parts of our daily lives. Yet the first comprehensive dictionary of the English language was published little more than two hundred and fifty years ago.

Throughout the seventeenth century, a number of small dictionaries appeared, but the purpose of these was to define and suggest usage for only difficult words, usually ones which had recently entered the English language and thus needed explanation. The best of these was *New World of Words* by Edward Phillips, a dictionary first published in 1658 and which reached its seventh edition by 1720. However, a far more comprehensive work was published the following year; this was the *Universal Etymological English Dictionary* by Nathaniel Bailey, which was expanded in 1730 and then called *Dictionarium Britannicum.* It was a useful reference book, far superior in its scope to its predecessors.

Though Bailey's book contained more words, it was

surpassed in importance by Samuel Johnson's A *Dictionary of the English Language*, first published in 1755. Dr. Johnson's book was a monumental work, one that would remain the most important authority on the English language for one hundred years. It is remarkable in that it is largely the work of one man, who chose the words to be included, defined them, explained their derivations, and selected quotations to illustrate their usage. His sources for these forty thousand words were other dictionaries, conversational usage, and his own readings.

Johnson's aim in compiling his dictionary was to set a standard of correctness. He did not mean to "fix" the language. Recognizing the need for a constantly changing language, he merely wanted to slow down change so that the English of his day would not become obsolete in a short period of time. Words and their meanings would, of course, change. "Their changes," he wrote, "will be almost always informing us that language is the work of man, a being from whom permanence and stability cannot be expected."

Browsing through his dictionary today is a great source of pleasure. He makes fun of the Scottish assistants who helped him with the dictionary by defining *oats* as "a grain which in England is generally given to horses but in Scotland supports the people." His own personal opinions are expressed in definitions such as the one of *opera*—"an exotic and irrational entertainment." Some of his definitions require many more definitions; for example, *network* is "any thing reticulated or decussated, at equal distances, with interstices between the intersections"; a *blister* is "a pustule formed by raising the cuticle from the cutis, and filled with serous blood."

Other of Johnson's definitions reflect changing times. His first definition of *magazine* is "a storehouse, commonly an arsenal or armoury, or repository of provisions," while the second definition is "of late this word has signified a miscellaneous pamphlet." Johnson labeled the word *deft* obsolete, and disapproved of the words *belabour, cajole, gambler, touchy,* and *volunteer,* all of which are commonly used today. On the other hand, his dictionary includes *beclip* (which meant *embrace*), *nim* (*steal*), and *yclad* (*clothed*), all of which have since disappeared from the vocabulary.

Johnson's dictionary is the work of a man greatly concerned with his language. It is also a work which gave great pleasure in its time (the poet Robert Browning is said to have read it from cover to cover), and browsing through it today can provide many insights into our language and how it has changed in the course of a few hundred years.

Another English-language dictionary of great importance was published across the ocean—in the United States—in 1828. The work of another man greatly concerned with his language, an American scholar, Noah Webster, it was called *An American Dictionary of the English Language,* and the emphasis was on the word

American. Webster believed, as did many scholars of this new nation, that the language spoken in America could be distinguished from that used in England. He began writing of these distinctions in the late eighteenth century, and his dictionary, which contained twelve thousand words not found in Johnson's, set down standards of uniquely American usage, pronunciation, and spelling.

That Johnson's and Webster's dictionaries remained popular for many decades is a tribute to their extraordinary usefulness. But by the second half of the nineteenth century, even these reference books were proving to be inadequate. After seriously investigating the problems of language, the Philological Society of London came to the conclusion that there was a need for a new, comprehensive dictionary. The aim of this projected dictionary was to record every word which could be found in the English language from about the year 1000 to the present time. It would include the history of each form of each word and all of its uses and meanings, past and present. A vast number of quotations would illustrate the historical evolution in meanings. This new dictionary would be the all-inclusive, definitive work on the subject.

In 1884, after many years of preparation, the first part of this dictionary, which went through part of the letter A, was issued. Sixteen years later, in 1900, work through the letter *H* was concluded, and in 1928, the dictionary was completed. The *Oxford English Dictionary* at that time comprised ten volumes, with 15,487 pages; there were 240,165 main entries. Other dictionaries have since surpassed it in size, but the *Oxford* remains a unique authority on the history and usage of the English language.

A Melting Pot

The vocabulary we use today can best be described as a melting pot. The term itself is defined as a country or city of any locality in which people of various races or nationalities are brought together and assimilated. Leafing through a good dictionary of the English language and looking up the derivations of our everyday words provide ample proof that our language itself is a melting pot, for it has brought together words from an enormous number of tongues, left them as they were or adapted them, and successfully assimilated them.

We use these words every day, and they come to us not only from Latin or German or French, but also from such exotic tongues as Tamil, Arawak, Sanskrit, and Turkish. The average person is probably unaware of it, but when he or she goes to the local supermarket, the shelves are filled with items whose names are derived from these and many other languages.

Bread is Old Norse in origin, *rye* and *pumpernickel* come from the German, but the *bagel* that might be found nearby is Yiddish. *Salt* and *eggs* are Old Norse, but the *bacon* to accompany the eggs comes from the French, while *coffee* is Arabic and *tea* is Chinese. *Toast* is French, but the *butter* we put on it comes from Latin, and the *marmalade* we might use is Portuguese in origin. *Yoghurt* is Turkish in origin and *ginger* comes from the Sanskrit. A *barbecue sauce?* That seemingly American word *barbecue* comes from Arawak, the language of the people who come from the Greater Antilles. *Sauce*, more understandably, comes from the French, who are known for their sauces. *Spaghetti*, of course, comes from the Italian, but it is found on many an American *menu* (that's French), and *cole slaw* and *cookies* are Dutch in origin. *Sauerkraut* and *pretzels* are originally German, so it's not surprising that we find them not only in the supermarket but also in the *delicatessen* (a German word that we've appropriated). The *potato* comes from the Spanish; *tapioca, squash,* and *pecan* are words we've acquired from the American Indians; and *curry* comes from the Tamil, a language of southern India and northern and eastern Ceylon.

Before dinner, the host or hostess might want to serve *whiskey*—that's Celtic—or perhaps *sherry*, which is Spanish, or *port*, which is Portuguese. And it was once customary for the women to adjourn to the drawing room—the origin of that is *with*drawing room—while the men enjoyed their *cigar*, which comes from the Spanish.

All of these words are now so much a part of the English language that they are completely accepted as English. They are indeed English, but it must be remembered that their origins are foreign.

New Meanings
for Old Words

The English language has never stood still. This is clear
from the way it has borrowed and assimilated words from
other languages and from the ways in which many words
have changed in meaning over the centuries.

The word *hybrid* is a colorful example. Today it means
something of mixed origin, but this word of Latin origin
once meant the offspring of a tame sow and a wild boar.
And before that, in Greek, it meant arrogance or ruth-
lessness.

Zest is another interesting example. Borrowed from

the French, it entered our language in the seventeenth century, and at first it meant lemon or orange peel. What originally gave additional flavor to nothing more than food or drink grew in meaning until this flavor—or enjoyment—was applied to every phase of life. Today we have a zest for learning, and traveling adds zest to our lives.

There are very many more examples of words which mean one thing today and meant other things in the past. When we now speak of a buxom woman, we think of one who is plump, healthy, and, more specifically, full-bosomed. However, when originally used in Old English, *buxom* meant easily bowed down or yielding. It came from the verb *bugan*, which meant "to bend or bow." During the years of Middle English, it was transformed into the adjective *buhsum*, which meant "pliant." "To be buxom" meant "to be obedient." In Shakespeare's times, one meaning was "full of life, or healthy." From that meaning came our modern usage, applied to well-endowed women alone.

A *pest* today is a nag or a nuisance, a troublesome person. But originally this word, which came from the French *peste*, was something far more serious, since it designated an epidemic, usually the bubonic plague. It wasn't merely irritating, as is today's pest; it was in most cases deadly.

Sleuth is another word that has changed radically in meaning. Today's sleuth is a detective, but originally a *sloth*, an Old Norse word, was a track or a trail. The word came into Middle English as *sleuth*, meaning the track of an animal or person. In a short time, it was used only in compounds such as *sleuth-dog*, meaning a dog trained to follow a track. In Scotland, a *sleuthhound* was a kind of bloodhound used to seek out criminals. In the nineteenth century, Americans began to call detectives "sleuthhounds," and in time the term was shortened to *sleuth*.

An *assassin* was once anyone who chewed or smoked hashish; *rheumatism* once meant a cold in the head; and a *rascal* was a young deer in poor condition. We find such fascinating pieces of information on almost every page of the dictionary, proof of the flexibility of our language.

In general, most students of language have placed changes in word meaning in four different categories. One category includes words which have narrowed in meaning, in which a general term has developed into a specific one. For example, *meat* once meant any food; *deer* was a general term for any animal; a *wife* was any woman, not necessarily a married one, and if people were *starving* it didn't mean that they merely lacked food but that they were dying.

The second category is the opposite of this—words that have widened in meaning, a specific term having developed into a more general one. A *butcher* was no more than a slaughterer of goats, a *place* was no more than a wide street or open square, and a *yen* was a specific craving for narcotics. The meanings of these words have expanded and been generalized. *Quarantine* has an especially interesting history, coming into English from the Latin, via French, and acquiring an infinitely more general meaning in the process. *Quadraginta*, the original Latin word meaning *forty*, became *quarante* in French. So *quarantine* was once a period of exactly forty days during which time a ship suspected of carrying contagious disease was not allowed to have contact with shore. Today *quarantine* means the restriction itself; it no longer has anything to do with shipboard diseases, nor is it used to specify a period of forty days.

A number of words, too, acquired broader meanings when the English language came into contact with American soil. In England, a *rock* had been a large mass of mineral material; in America the term was applied to small stones as well. In England, a *barn* was a place in which to store nothing but crops; in America it became a place to keep cattle as well. To *haul* for the English meant to move by force; in America something transported by any vehicle was hauled. And the word *mad*, too, which meant insane in England, came to mean not only that but angry as well when imported into America.

The other two categories include words whose meanings have either been degraded or elevated in status. For example, a *harlot* in Chaucer's time was an innocent servant—it did not have today's derogatory meaning; a *villain* was a serf or peasant and not someone evil; and a *lewd* person was not depraved or lascivious but merely untaught or ignorant. To call someone *puny* today is an insult compared to the earlier meaning of the word, which was "younger." These are examples of words which have been degraded in meaning.

Other words have been elevated or enhanced in meaning. Today's *pioneer* is a man of courage and vision; a *pioneer* was once nothing more than a common infantry soldier who specialized in digging trenches. *Nice* is a rather weak and vague adjective today, but it is certainly complimentary; yet in the past it has meant ignorant, then foolish, then shy, and finally discriminating, before its current definition as agreeable or pleasant. A *banquet* was once not the huge and festive meal it is today; it was merely a light refreshment served between meals.

Proper Nouns into Common Words

Very often, words have been the product of man's imagination and resourcefulness, as when they have been created by combining already existing words (*smog* and *motel*), or coined to imitate sounds (*bang* and *pop*).

A study of word origins teaches us, too, that many of our words are derived from proper nouns—from the names of people who have achieved a certain fame or notoriety, from the names of gods, and from the names of places.

For example, there was the case of Nicolas Chauvin,

a very patriotic man. A soldier in Napoleon's army, he loved his leader and his country. He was so devoted to them that all people who showed excessive love for their country became known as *chauvinists*.

Etienne de Silhouette, another Frenchman, was his country's minister of finance in the middle of the eighteenth century. He carefully watched government expenditures and imposed strict taxes on the nobility. His fanatical stinginess was such that a cheap person became known as a *silhouette*. Later he was ridiculed, and spare, unadorned outline drawings—with no extra detail—became known as *silhouettes*. They are still known as such today; they are bare outlines.

There are other interesting and commonly used words that came into our language through their association with literary figures. Leopold von Sacher-Masoch was a well-known nineteenth-century German novelist who wrote about a man who found pleasure in being abused by the one he loved. He gave us the words *masochist* and *masochism*. The words *sadist* and *sadism* owe their existence to an infamous French nobleman, the Marquis de Sade, who in the eighteenth century described not the joys of receiving but the pleasures of giving punishment.

John Montagu, the fourth Earl of Sandwich (1718–1792), was addicted to gambling. Rather than stop his favorite activity for lunch or dinner, he would eat pieces of cold meat placed between two slices of bread.

Because of this, an important word and a way of eating entered our vocabulary. Charles C. Boycott, a British army officer and landowner who lived in the nineteenth century, was hated by those who rented property from him because he made them pay too much. To retaliate, these tenants refused to pay any rent at all. Their method of retaliation has been adopted and adapted by many groups since that time, and a boycott is today a commonly used method of coercion and intimidation.

A *cardigan* is a sweater-jacket, named after James Thomas Brudenell, the seventh Earl of Cardigan, who led the Charge of the Light Brigade in the nineteenth century. *Lynch* is derived from the *Lynch law*—named after a Virginian named Lynch who lived in the eighteenth century. The nineteenth-century Austrian doctor, F. A. Mesmer, hypnotized through animal magnetism. Today a person who is spellbound or hypnotized is mesmerized.

Gods also have provided us with common nouns. Atlas was one of the giants of Greek mythology, whose duty was to hold up the sky. A Flemish mapmaker published a book of maps in the sixteenth century with a drawing of Atlas on the title page. He titled this collection of maps *Atlas*, and before long an *atlas* was any book of maps. *Panic* is another example, a word derived from the ancient Greek god Pan who instilled fear and terror into the enemy during battle.

Places, too, are the sources for many common nouns.

46

The word *attic* is derived from the region of ancient Greece called Attica, and its elegant architectural style known as Attic. A *milliner* was originally a man who sold goods from the Italian city of Milan. And the origins of the word for our unit of currency, the *dollar*, are surprisingly not American at all. Instead, this familiar word comes from the name of a Bohemian town called Jachymov. This seems a long way from *dollar*, but it really isn't. In the early sixteenth century, the town was known by its German name of Sankt Joachimsthal. This was the site of a silver mine which minted coins known as *joachimstaler*. This word was shortened to *taler* and then became *daler* in Dutch. Soon this word was taken into English to refer to certain coins, and on July 6, 1785, Congress passed a resolution that "the money unit of the United States of America be one dollar."

Chauvinist, silhouette, masochist, sadist, sandwich, cardigan—these and other words are but a few examples of the ways in which man's ingenuity has led to the enrichment of the English language.

Euphemisms: Don't Say What You Mean

Jack Worthing, a character in Oscar Wilde's *The Importance of Being Earnest*, tells his questioner that he has "lost" both of his parents. The reply is an irritated: "To lose one parent may be regarded as a misfortune— to lose both seems like carelessness."

The questioner thought Worthing meant his parents were dead, but instead of using the unpleasant word *dead* he had substituted for it the word *lost*, a more delicate way of expressing a harsh fact; he had used a euphemism, a word or phrase to soften the impact of a harsh or embarrassing word, the substitute word or phrase being either milder or less embarrassing. The word *euphemism* itself comes from the Greek: *eu*, which means good or well; and *phem*, which means to speak. Its ancestor is the Greek word *euphēmes*, "sounding good," and a euphemism is a way of using our language to *not* say exactly what we mean.

With the aid of euphemisms, a large number of real names for what might be considered indecent or improper or just unpleasant are disguised and replaced with what might be considered less objectionable names. A surprising number of them are used to cover up the basic truths of life and of death.

The word *death* itself and the whole concept of dying have been so disguised for many centuries. In the time of Old English, one spoke not of someone's death but rather of a journey or a departure. Shakespeare wrote that one character "surceased," that another was "put to silence," and that another "took off." He meant that they were dead.

In our time, just as in Oscar Wilde's, we "lose" a friend or a relative. People "pass away" or are "no longer among the living." Some "go to their reward"—they are then not among the dead but among the "departed."

Once "departed," they are looked after by an "undertaker." An "undertaker" was once any person who undertook a job or a task; a funeral undertaker arranged funerals, but the term *funeral undertaker* seemed too depressing, and so a funeral undertaker became merely an undertaker. That, too, in time became unpleasant, and the "undertaker" often became a "funeral director." In America now, a seemingly more dignified term, *mortician*, is often preferred.

Other terms associated with death, too, have changed. Many "funeral parlors" are now "chapels," and instead of "cemeteries" many of those who are "no longer among the living" are buried in "memorial parks." Death is a harsh reality, a truth which people have for many centuries tried to disguise by means of euphemisms.

Disease is also something to be disguised. Until very recently the ugly word—ugly only because it described something ugly—*cancer* was commonly substituted by the word *malignancy*. And for centuries people suffered not from "tuberculosis" but from "consumption."

Old age, too, is presumably considered something to be hidden. The old are, in fact, no longer "old," they are "senior citizens." They receive "retirement allowances" instead of "old-age pensions," and "old folks' homes" have disappeared, replaced by "retirement villages."

Direct mention of the acts of urination and defecation has long been avoided, though they are obviously normal and healthy functions of our daily lives. We ask for and go to a "john," or a "comfort station," or a "men's room," or a "ladies' room." A woman goes to a "powder room" not necessarily to powder her nose, and we go to the "rest room" when we don't want to rest. We want to know where the "bathroom" is when we have no intention of taking a bath, and we seek the "lavatory" when we don't want to wash—as the word implies. "Do you want to wash your hands?" or "Do you want to powder your nose?" are questions commonly asked by a polite host or hostess who in that way avoids simply asking if anyone wants to use the toilet.

It is perhaps understandable that euphemisms are often used for any of the subjects mentioned above, but it is difficult to understand the use of disguises for the state of being pregnant. Nonetheless, women are "expecting," they are "expectant mothers" and are "in the family way." Some are in an "interesting condition," this latter derived from an Italian way of describing the condition of being pregnant.

More understandable are the uses of euphemisms for what we now call "mental illness," or "mental disorders." People are no longer "insane" or "crazy"—they are "disturbed," "unbalanced," or "pathological." They are not sent as they once were to an "insane asylum," but to a "mental hospital." And very recently psychiatrists lost their "patients." They now have "clients."

On a social level, the "poor" are now "underprivileged," members of the "lower income brackets." And "underdeveloped" nations must have taken offense at that adjective, for while they were first "underdeveloped," they are now "developing."

Euphemisms are very often used to raise the status of one's profession or occupation. "Real estate agents" are often "realtors," just as many "hairdressers" have become "beauticians," and "barbers" nowadays are often known as "stylists." "Gardeners" are "tree surgeons" or "landscape architects," and people who go from store to store to sell books are not "traveling salesmen" but merely "book travelers," probably to set them apart from those salespeople who sell less worthy merchandise.

In recent years there have been great changes in the names given to people who do domestic work. In the past few decades the word *servant*, except in extreme cases, has disappeared. Its connotation was a decidedly unpleasant and undemocratic one. Other changes, however, are of little real importance. A "nurse" for a baby is now most likely a "mother's helper," and most people no longer hire "maids"—they engage "help" or a "house-keeper."

There are other kinds of euphemisms, such as those which replace holy names "used in vain," or words that at one time or another were not to be used in polite company. Among the former are *golly* or *gosh*, instead of *God*, and *gee* and *gee whiz* to replace *Jesus*. Among the latter are *darn* and *dash* to replace *damn*, and *shoot*, *shucks*, and *sugar* to substitute for *shit*.

Fashions change in words as in many other facets of our lives, and a study of euphemisms tells us much about our society and our own psychological makeup. It is enough to point out that euphemisms were once created to replace everyday and, to us, harmless words such as *leg* and *trouser*—both once considered embarrassing terms—to understand that our values and ideas have changed as drastically as has our language in the course of our history. It is interesting, too, to note that many euphemisms in time have so convincingly replaced the so-called unpleasant words that they were meant to disguise that they themselves had to be replaced—with further euphemisms. *Whore,* for example, was once a euphemism for a now-forgotten word, and *cemetery* was originally a polite substitute for *graveyard.*

Some of these euphemisms seem to us far-fetched and exaggerated, means of hiding facts and concepts that should be faced. Yet it cannot be denied that they, too, have helped in their way to enlarge our vocabulary and enrich the English language.

Slang

Euphemisms are used to soften the impact of what we are saying. Other terms, known as slang—colorful words and sometimes strikingly imaginative phrases—are used to intensify the impact of what we are describing.

Take the simple sentence: "They had too much to drink and got drunk." Using slang, we might say that they went on a *spree*, a *toot*, a *jag*, a *bender*, or a *binge*.

As a result, we could say they were *high*, *lit*, *plastered*, or *stiff*. They were *tipsy* and they were *loaded* or they were *stewed*. They were also *blotto, in their cups, blind,* or *pie-eyed*. In addition, they were *tight, soused, sizzled, pickled*, or *three sheets in the wind*. They were *woozy*. . . .

These terms might not be polite, but for centuries men have done their best to find new and more colorful terms to describe acts that could already be adequately—if not interestingly—described by already existing words. Indeed, this invention of new words or combinations of old words as substitutes for conventional vocabulary is as old as language itself. Benjamin Franklin, in his time, compiled a list of 228 terms for *drunk*—and today, two hundred years later, a slang dictionary lists almost one thousand terms which describe the same condition.

Nonetheless, slang, so much a part of our everyday means of communication, has often been treated as a vaguely illegitimate child of our "proper" language. It has been looked down upon and scorned, and often only grudgingly accepted as "nonstandard" English. But slang will always be a part of the English language.

This "nonstandard" vocabulary is formed in many ways; one of the simplest and most obvious is the shortening of accepted words. "The doc and the prof left the lab, got on their bikes, and went to the gym. . . . "

Less obvious, because the shortened words are now so commonly used that they have actually replaced the originals and can no longer be thought of as slang (though they are), are words such as *taxi, bus*, and *cab*. Certainly no one today would think of asking for a taximeter, omnibus, or cabriolet—the original, preslang terms for these means of transportation. And some short-ened words once thought of as slang have strayed so far from their originals that they are hardly recognizable: *pep* came from *pepper*, and *fan* was short for *fanatic*.

Unconventional descriptions, often figures of speech or metaphors, are sometimes the source of slang words and expressions. A few of these are concerned with the characteristics of the human head. A man or woman with a high brow was thought to be cultured—therefore, the word *highbrow*. And along with it came the words *lowbrow* (little cultured) and *middlebrow* (somewhere between the two). In 1952, a highbrow named Adlai Stevenson ran for the office of President of the United States. Because Stevenson was balding, he and the sup-porters of this unusually erudite politician became known as eggheads, because of the presumed resemblance of the shape of the candidate's head to that of an egg. In a short time, the word *egghead* was used to describe any intel-lectual.

There are a large number of colorful metaphors that have entered our language as slang and have remained a permanent part of our vocabulary because of their apt-ness in describing conditions or situations. An unstable or deranged personality has a *screw loose* or *bats in the belfry*. We have, for very many years, gone *out on a limb, passed the buck, hit the road*, and been *left holding the bag*. These slang expressions are so vivid that no dictionary is needed to define them.

Slang is also created by taking old standard words and combining them to make new meanings. We recognize the meaning of *bigwig, big shot, big wheel*, or a *big man*—none of these has anything to do with physical size when used as slang. *Spaced* and *out* have recently been combined to give a new meaning, as have *rip* and *off* and *put* and *on*.

A very large number of conventional old words, too, have been given new meanings and thereby converted into slang. We *dig* things without a shovel, and we keep our *cool* even on the hottest days without the aid of air conditioning. We don't have to *split* pieces of wood or anything when we use that verb as slang, and we *split* our sides with laughter without any need for surgery.

Until recently, *speed* meant velocity, *grass* and *weed* were part of every field, *pot* was something to cook in, and *acid* was a chemical term; then they all acquired new meanings in terms of the drug *scene*—the word *scene* in this sense having nothing to do with the theatre.

Some words are so commonly used as slang that their original meaning almost disappears. Nowadays when someone is called *gay*, we assume that that person is homosexual and not necessarily happy and lighthearted. In this case our language has been impoverished and not enriched by the use of a slang expression.

Many books have been written about slang, and many dictionaries of slang are available. The first serious one, A *Classical Dictionary of the Vulgar Tongue*, was published as long ago as 1785. The origins of some terms are obscure—they might have been coined and used by a journalist or a politician—and others can be carefully traced. All, however, are the product of man's desire to enrich the language by revolting against its formalities, and making it more lively and picturesque. At first, slang words and expressions might be the exclusive property of any single related group, their use serving as a kind of badge of membership in that group. But those words that prove to be of value beyond the limits of that group become more generalized and remain as part of the everyday language of people outside that group.

Slang is certainly, in most cases, ephemeral—that is, most slang terms have a period during which they are in fashion, then they disappear and become reminders of the past. Nonetheless, a large number of words have entered our vocabulary as slang and have subsequently become part of our standard language.

When Shakespeare used the words *fireworks*, *fretful*, and *dwindle*, he was using slang. Samuel Johnson, in the eighteenth century, was offended by the use of such slang terms as *gambler* and *frisky*. In that century, too, *bored* was considered a slang word to be avoided by all serious writers. The word *sweater* was thought of as slang in 1880, and at one time or another all of the following words were considered to be slang: *swagger, tidy, blizzard, until, encroach, clumsy, strenuous, joke, freshman,* and *glib*. There were, surely, other words with meanings equivalent to these, but these new slang words proved so successful that they either replaced or supplemented them. They are today legitimate members of our vocabulary and would not be out of place in even the most scholarly journal.

Another group of slang words or expressions has persisted and remained in use for long periods of time, but the words have never changed their status as slang. Shakespeare wrote *beat it, done me wrong, fall for it,* and *not so hot:* these were slang expressions in his day, as they are today. Chaucer referred to dice as "bones," a still popular word, but one that has never been accepted by dictionaries as more than slang. *Gab,* too, a word Chaucer used, has met with the same fate. *To cough up,* as we *cough up* money, was slang in the sixteenth century, just as it is now. A *sap* was a fool two hundred years ago, just as a *sap* is a fool today—yet the word has still not been accepted as part of conventional speech.

Beat meant worn out and exhausted in 1830, and a *wolf* was a seducer in 1858. *Grapevine* was coined at the time of the American Civil War, when it was given the meaning of an unofficial rumor, derived from the twisting tendrils of a grapevine. The word and its meaning have remained the same, yet it has not yet been promoted to the status of standard language by most dictionaries.

If we describe a pretty girl as a *piece* or a *broad,* we think we're *with it,* to use another slang expression. Yet a pretty girl was called a *piece* in the fourteenth century, and she was referred to as a *broad* in the sixteenth century.

Nonetheless, if that same pretty girl were called a *pip*, a *wow*, a *wench*, or a *skirt*, there would be some question as to the meaning of the terms, for these once popular slang expressions are rarely, if ever, used today. But it is certainly interesting to note that though many terms were coined to describe a woman as a sex object, there are few such equivalents to describe a man. Psychological and social factors are reflected in slang.

There is no doubt that most slang, no matter how popular it is, is short-lived, because social and psychological conditions change rapidly. In this last quarter of the twentieth century, we get *vibes*, we *do our act*, and we *get it together*. Some of us are described as *workaholics*. Quite probably, none of these expressions will survive this decade, or even this year. Nonetheless, there is no doubt that slang is an important part of our language. It stretches our imagination, it stimulates us to seek new ways of saying old things, and it might, as we have seen, permanently enrich our vocabulary.

The Future
of the Language

What is the future of the English language? No one can say, but because it is both alive and very healthy it will inevitably continue to grow and change as long as it is used. By now rules of basic grammar have been fixed, though there will be slight variations which will be accepted because of usage or misusage. Our basic vocabulary, too, will remain the same, but there is no doubt that a reader one hundred years from now will be astounded at some of the definitions found in our contemporary dictionaries—and even more astounded at the omission of words which are, or seem to be, a solid part of his or her vocabulary.

Because people from countries in which other languages are spoken will continue to visit and sometimes settle in our English-speaking lands, they will continue to bring with them some words which we English-speaking people find useful to add to our vocabulary.

Slang will, by its very nature, change. Words and phrases popular today will, for the most part, disappear and be replaced by other words and phrases which will, too, for the most part, disappear.

People will continue to lend their names to new concepts or new objects: there was no Freudian slip before Freud, nor was there an Eisenhower jacket before Eisenhower. Our ever-inventive minds, too, will think of new euphemisms to conceal the unpleasant facts of life.

Usage will also change. We need only think how the once respectable word *Negro* has only recently become unacceptable, replaced by the word *black*, which itself was once unacceptable. New terminologies enter our language and are accepted quickly—*Ms.* as a replacement for *Miss* or *Mrs.* has become standard almost overnight, as has *chairperson* to replace *chairman*, and similar rapid changes will undoubtedly occur with regularity.

The changes in the field of technology will be even more startling, especially in the areas of electronics and space travel and medicine. Each new invention or discovery will call for a new word, just as new words will be essential to describe hitherto unknown concepts. Our language will have no difficulty in meeting these challenges by drawing on its past. Not so long ago, there was no such word as *astronaut,* so we simply put together two recognizable roots—*astro* and *naut.*

One change in our language that can be predicted is that the form of English spoken in America, because of its wide acceptance throughout the world, will become increasingly popular—as compared to the form of English spoken in Great Britain.

Since the seventeenth century, when the first British colonists settled in America, differences have emerged between what we might call American English and British English. Since that time, there has been a kind of war between these two forms of the language. For a long time, the British considered the Americans upstarts; they felt that contact with the New World was corrupting the pure English language, and they criticized what they thought of as "crude Americanisms." Nonetheless, the Americans continued to respond to the challenges of their new country and their new way of life by changing and adding to the language as they saw fit. In time, much to the dismay of English purists, many of these Americanisms even found their way back to, and became popular in, England.

Fortunately, this futile and unproductive war has come to an end over the past thirty years. American books, movies, and television programs are so popular in England that their language has successfully invaded "pure" English. Many English scholars have come to America, just as many American scholars have gone to England. The scholars have so influenced one another that their languages are almost indistinguishable. Tourism has increased, and the interchange between Americans and English is so great that it is often hard to tell which word or phrase was originally English and which was originally American. Undoubtedly, because of the influence of American entertainment and writing as well as the vast presence of American soldiers in England both during and after World War II, more Americanisms have entered the English language than recent English inventions have entered the American English. But often we're not sure, and we tend to forget that *I've had it, take a dim view of,* and *opposite number* are examples of Anglicisms that have been adopted by Americans. Nonetheless, if only because of the large number of its speakers, the American brand of English predominates in today's world, and will most likely continue to do so.

Differences remain. Americans live in *apartments* rather than in *flats;* they take *elevators* to get there, while the English take *lifts.* Americans eat *candy* between meals and *dessert* at the end of a meal; the English have a *sweet* at the end of the meal and *sweets* at other times. American *French fried potatoes* are English *chips,* and Americans buy *canned* food while the English buy *tinned* food. When traveling, the English buy a *single*

64

ticket or a *return*, while the Americans buy *round trip* or *one way*. An American will fill his *truck* with *gas*, and an Englishman fills his *lorry* with *petrol*. And finally, and more confusingly, an English *public* school is actually, as far as Americans are concerned, a *private* school.

These remaining differences are, at worst, minor. Sometimes they are amusing inconveniences. It is no longer true that "England and America are two countries separated by the same language," as George Bernard Shaw once wrote. Instead, their similarities are so great that they might be considered, in the words of Alexander Pope, "parts of one stupendous whole." That whole, the English language, will continue to change and grow and marvelously serve our needs to express ourselves and communicate with one another.

Bibliography

ALEXANDER, HENRY. *The Story of Our Language.* New York: Thomas Nelson & Sons, 1940.

BAUGH, ALBERT C. *A History of the English Language.* New York: Appleton-Century-Crofts, 1957.

BLOOMFIELD, MORTON W. *Language.* New York: Holt, Rinehart and Winston, 1933.

BROOK, G. L. *A History of the English Language.* New York: W. W. Norton, 1958.

DILLARD, J. L. *All-American English.* New York: Random House, 1975.

————. *Black English*. New York: Random House, 1972.

FARB, PETER. *Word Play*. New York: Alfred A. Knopf, Inc., 1974.

FOWLER, H. W. *A Dictionary of Modern English Usage*. 2d ed. New York: Oxford University Press, 1965.

JESPERSEN, OTTO. *Growth and Structure of the English Language*. New York: Thomas Nelson & Sons, 1905.

KRAPP, G. P. *The English Language in America*. New York: Appleton-Century-Crofts, 1925.

MENCKEN, H. L. *The American Language*. New York: Alfred A. Knopf, Inc., 1948.

PARTRIDGE, ERIC. *A Dictionary of Slang and Unconventional English*. New York: Macmillan, 1970.

PEI, MARIO. *The Story of the English Language*. Philadelphia: J. B. Lippincott, 1967.

————. *The Story of Language*. Philadelphia: J. B. Lippincott, 1965.

POTTER, SIMEON. *Our Language*. Baltimore: Penguin Books, 1964.

SAPIR, EDWARD. *Selected Writings*. Edited by D. G. Mandelbaum. Berkeley: University of California Press, 1949.